Footsteps in Paradise!

FOOTSTEPS IN PARADISE!

Sheilah Daughtree BA, ALAA

Footsteps in Paradise!
Sheilah Daughtree
Edited by Daphne van Loenen

Published by Greyhound Self-Publishing 2022
Malvern, Worcestershire, United Kingdom.

Printed and bound by Aspect Design
89 Newtown Road, Malvern, Worcs. WR14 1PD United Kingdom
Tel: 01684 561567 • E-mail: allan@aspect-design.net
Website: www.aspect-design.net

Cover Design Copyright © 2022 Aspect Design
Cover photo: Longreach Art Centre
Original images Copyright © 2022 Lynn Cooke

ISBN 978-1-909219-92-2

CONTENTS

Chapter I
BEGINNINGS

The worst Christmas present I ever gave my parents was in 1964 when I announced I was going to Australia with husband RJ and children. Mum was shocked but didn't show it. Instead she just said, "You won't like it you know" in a rather subdued voice, and my dad said nothing.

"It's quite civilised." I said rather glibly. "They have all the things over there that we have here and we want some warmth and sunshine after last year's winter." How wrong I was about it all, but I was going to find out the hard way.

My Aunt and Uncle had been in Brisbane for a few years. Letters back and forth and the Australian government's advertising drive to encourage people to try for a new life prompted us to look seriously at emigrating. We were both doing two jobs and with two young children to bring up we thought the time was right for a change. We decided to go by sea so that we could have a holiday on the ship – a cruise for five weeks – but it didn't turn out quite as we planned.

With many tears and last minute misgivings we said good-bye to my parents as we boarded the train, very unhappy but also excited at the same time. In Southampton we met friends for lunch but it was rather a sad time and it was drizzling with rain, much like our mood. We trailed around for a while with their three children and our two just killing time and not really knowing how to say goodbye. It was too late to change our minds, everything had been sold and what we had left was on the ship.

Our friends stayed to see us depart and we waved a sad farewell from the deck with bright streamers flying from ship to shore. Finally the coloured streamers parted and fell into the water as the ship moved away from the dock. All we could think about was whether we would ever see any of our family and friends again. The other side of the world in 1965 was more like going to another planet with a space ship that may not call again.

Although we had been given a cabin number with our paper work for the trip when we boarded the ship, our accommodation was reallocated to us and we found ourselves in two separate cabins a long way apart. I was in a four-berth cabin with a lady from Kenya, her sixteen-year-old daughter my six-year-old son and nearly four-year-old daughter. In the centre of the cabin was a cot. None of us could move around and had to take turns in standing up to get dressed or using the minute bathroom.

Worse was to come when my daughter took one look at the cot and, screaming, flatly refused to go near it and I was battling to keep my dinner down. In the end I put the mattress from the cot on the floor and put the cot outside the steward's room. By the time I had settled my daughter I succumbed to my rising nausea. RJ said we hadn't even left Southampton waters.

The couple from Kenya were most considerate as I tried to keep to a routine with the children when I could stand up, and they even cleaned up my son when he was sick and I couldn't stand. Their kindness we will always remember.

Over the next few days RJ appeared from his cabin and took charge of the children as seasickness left me in no doubt that standing up was not a good thing to do. They very quickly found their way around the ship without going outside and could safely take themselves off to breakfast and to children's club for the mornings. I tried from time to time to make the decks outside for some fresh air. Mostly I managed about half an hour before seasickness overtook me again. This was not turning out to be the cruise I had imagined.

Our very tall Chinese steward was extremely kind and constantly came up with special drinks and food that I could keep down, and amused my children and other children from the corridor in his pantry from time to time. I finally made it to the Italian Doctor who just looked at me and in fractured English asked if I was pregnant!

My daughter, Jane-Ann, had her fourth birthday on the ship. We had a large sponge cake made for her but also enough for the other children who were at her party. Our Chinese steward gave her a small but beautifully carved ebony and ivory elephant. A most unusual present for a four-year-old and from someone we didn't know at all. She carried the Elephant everywhere but it never had a name. I realised one day that she no longer had it with her in her little pink cloth bag. I was devastated with the loss because I think the Elephant was perhaps one of our Chinese steward's only possessions. I put out a plea to the Purser that it was a child's birthday present and if found, could they please return it. Being such a small item I had little hope of ever seeing it again and worried how I could tell our steward it was lost. Within hours someone found it and reunited the Elephant with my daughter. Today 'Elephant' sits in a special place in my daughter's house.

Seasickness was to haunt me for almost all the five weeks we were on board. My only respite was a few days in Egypt whilst the ship went through the Suez Canal. A trip was being organised to Cairo from the ship but we were advised not to take children, not only because it was very hot, but also because there was some unrest in the country. (Just before the Six Days War) RJ stayed to look after the children and about 40 of us set off for Cairo.

Chapter II
EGYPT

I was so excited to see a little something of Egypt, the fascinating country of the Pharaohs that I had only read about, and would perhaps never get the chance to see again. We were told to take water and fruit from the ship for our journey and not to eat fruit from the market vendors as they sometimes injected water, possibly contaminated water, into the fruit to make them juicy.

I met up with Caroline who was also on her own and we shared a room. (She was returning from her family in Austria to her husband in New Zealand – she was not an emigrant but a paying passenger). As we were the only two 'single' girls the Officer from our ship and the Egyptian Guide took us under their wings. They insisted on us sharing a table for dinner and ordering a special lamb dish for us along with an ice-cold Egyptian beer. Both were delicious. After such a long journey and wonderful meal we were escorted to the local gardens and there sat under the stars and listened to soft music while illuminated lights filled the sky with wonderful patterns. A beautiful end to the day.

Although extremely hot in Cairo I ignored the heat and was thrilled with my first taste of the exotic. Our hotel was in one of the main streets and looking out of the window was a world of brightly coloured shop awnings, dusty roads with cars, plodding donkeys and people in flowing coloured garments. The heat hit me like a wall as we stepped outside the first morning and onto the coach to take us to the Pyramids – and a ride on a camel. I had mistakenly worn a white cotton skirt and T-shirt. The colour was all right but the skirt was straight and getting on a camel was a sight to behold, especially for the camel driver! A photograph of this event was pinned up on the notice board in the ship when we returned, much to my embarrassment.

I survived the ride and climbed up to enter the tomb. For some reason the group from the ship was ahead of me so when I entered the pyramid I was alone. I managed about 50 yards into the dim humid passage with its huge block of grey/cream stones taller than me all around. The tunnel sloped upwards and curved round a sharp bend where there was a very feeble light. I turned the corner and seeing no one in front of me or hearing anything I simply froze and felt crushed at the same time. Holding myself against the wall I kept muttering to myself that it couldn't fall down and not to be silly. Sweat poured down my face and arms, far more than the temperature warranted and I just couldn't go any further.

I crawled back to the entrance and was promptly sick. More embarrassment as the camel drivers just looked at me and turned away. Shaking I sat outside the entrance to the tomb until everyone came back. It was my first experience of claustrophobia.

Cairo Museum was next on the morning's list to see the

wonders of the tomb of Tutankhamun. At this time very few artefacts had ever been outside Egypt. There was just so much to see and wonder at the remarkable workmanship. It was obvious that when Tutankhamun was buried everything he ever had was buried with him.

It was only much later in life when I studied Egyptology at university that I found out that someone had tried very hard to eliminate Tutankhamun from all the records. Perhaps that was the reason his tomb was never found until 1922? I was stunned by the masks of his face to the final one of gold which took my breath away. There were far too many artefacts to take in at one visit.

Our next stop was to be a perfume factory but Caroline and I rebelled and excused ourselves to stay longer in the Museum and find our own way back to the Hotel. We spent a magical afternoon not only looking at more of the splendid gold masks and funeral accoutrements of Tutankhamun but also his ordinary things such as his toy soldiers, (Roman) set out in various uniforms and units, board games, baby shoes and his childhood chairs, varying in size as he grew. On the way out we passed between the two black life-size standing wooden statues that had been found guarding his tomb and whose painted life-like eyes bored into mine as we passed. A very eerie experience.

We had time to inspect – with some apprehension – the body of the Pharaoh, Rameses II, some magnificent jewellery, painted walls and wooden statues from a variety of tombs, intricately wrapped mummies with painted faces on the bandaging and some stunning pottery. We finally dragged ourselves away wanting to see more and promising ourselves that one-day we would go back.

We had a map to guide us back to the hotel with strict instructions not to wander from the main road. We peeped into shops selling fine silk fabrics and cushions, highly polished brass trays with intricate beaten designs on low tables. Other shops had stuffed leather camel-like chairs, highly coloured and bedecked with brass trimmings. Shops had trays and jars of coloured spices whose aroma wafted towards us. The bright sunlight occasionally bounced off the windows and coloured fabrics of the little shops in the dark alleyways but, however tempting, we didn't venture inside.

After dinner that night Caroline and I were asked by our ship's Officer and the Egyptian Guide if we would like to go out to a nightclub in the desert. They were most courteous and kind and regaled us with funny stories and a little history of this fascinating country. The sky was a deep purple speckled with the first stars of the night against the dark outline of the pyramids on the horizon. Suddenly over a large sand dune emerged an enormous gold and red striped tent – was this the nightclub? Indeed it was, exactly like something out of the Arabian Nights. Twinkling lights and candles, low brass tables set with little pots of strange edibles! All surrounded by brightly coloured silk or wool cushions of every hue to sit on.

The centre was a plain wooden floor, and the walls were decorated with hangings and silk streamers that shimmered in the flickering lights. This was not any kind of nightclub I had seen before although I had actually worked at a cash desk in a night club in Brighton. The music was played with drums and stringed instruments, almost like lutes but with a very different sound. We sat and watched some fabulous dancing, mostly done by the men.

One dancer will forever live in my mind. He stood centre stage dressed in a loose-sleeved embroidered white shirt and long dark red skirt. With a single bright light in a sea of darkness he slowly began to rotate on the one spot. As he spun the music pulsed to his rhythm. Slowly he twirled faster and faster whilst at the same time taking hold of the skirt which had become a great red circle around the white shirt. As he became a whirling dervish the red skirt was lifted above his head like a giant umbrella. The sudden stop was electrifying as the red skirt enveloped him and the light went out.

The ladies who danced and shimmied to a pulsing beat were fully clothed but in sparkling layers of glittering flowing coloured silks and exotic jewellery. It was explained to us that these were special dancers who performed formally for Royalty and were not permitted to show much of the body. Small sweet drinks were served to us in minute thimble-like brass bowls by a white-coated waiter wearing red trousers and a red Fez. Finally we had to leave and walked into a desert devoid of any light. The sky was black and the stars so bright there seemed to be layer upon layer of them waiting to be touched. By the time we returned to Cairo it was 4 am and we decided an early breakfast at the Hilton was a good idea. They kindly supplied us with tea and toast before we made it back to our hotel.

After a rather short rest and a shower we were down for our second breakfast for 7 o'clock and then off to look at one of the largest and most beautiful mosques in Cairo with a panoramic view over the whole of the city. The only photograph I have is of a very blue sky and dun-coloured buildings on the horizon, but my memory is one of bright colours of the flowing robes of the men and women, the narrow streets with bright awnings and the smell of dust and spices. I loved every minute there.

As we were driven to Port Suez to reboard the ship we saw many troops lining the Suez Canal and in large transport convoys. It was just before the Six Days War with Israel but of course we didn't know that then. The sights, sounds and taste of Egypt were to remain with me for a very long time. Caroline and I both made a promise to return one day to a land that captivated us both. I haven't made it back, and I wonder if she has.

Aden was another adventure with bumboats plying their wares, baskets being hauled aboard with everything from fabric to leather goods and even a small table being lifted aloft. On the quayside were armed troops and we were warned not to stray too far away from the quay. We wandered the shops and bought a new electric shaver for RJ, and a lovely doll for our daughter's birthday – she was four as we crossed the Equator.

The night of the Equatorial dinner the stabilisers were put out and the ship was calm so I made it to the dinner – next to the top table! I even managed a dance but at midnight the stabilisers were removed and I didn't even manage to make it to the ladies toilet in time to be sick. I felt so embarrassed and never did find the people who looked after me that night to thank them.

Our first very tentative and rather staggering steps on dry land after Aden was the promised land of Australia, Fremantle to be precise. All we wanted was real milk and so did everyone else by the number of crates of milk lined up outside the dock gates. We stretched our legs with a walk up to the highest point at the War Memorial lookout. Our view was the docks, not quite the golden beaches I had expected to see. We made our way back to the ship and just as we reached the bottom of the hill I realised I had left all our coats behind. RJ sprinted back and just made it to the ship as the gangway was being dragged aboard.

In Melbourne we said goodbye to our cabin companions and to Caroline. Her husband had come to meet her with a very large bunch of flowers. We all had lunch in our first Australian restaurant and as we said goodbye she gave me the flowers as a reminder of our time together.

On the way back to the ship some luggage was still being unloaded. As we watched our very large distinguishable black trunk was being whisked onto the quay. We weren't getting off in Melbourne so why was our luggage? Dashing on to the ship we enquired where our luggage was going. We were told it was routine to offload Brisbane luggage in Melbourne! Our thoughts were sceptical and we wondered if we would ever see it again. It did indeed arrive safe and sound three months later!

Our next stop was Sidney and after battling the huge waves in the Great Australian Bight we sailed at night into calm waters and under the famous Harbour Bridge. Sydney was all around us with the twinkling lights of the city and the shrouded Sidney Opera House just off to the left of us. We sat on the deck that night looking at the lights of the famous city as a warm breeze wafted around us. Weeks on the boat had given us some idea of distance and we began to realise how far away we really were from home. We were not allowed off the ship and sailed early for our final stop, Brisbane. I promised myself one day to drive across the Sidney Harbour Bridge and indeed we did a few years later.

Chapter III
FIRST STEPS

I was still feeling rather sick as we arrived in Brisbane at 7am on a chilly Friday 13th of August. We could see my Aunt and Uncle with three of the children, Bobby, Jennifer and Victor, on the shore jumping up and down and waving a flag. Years later Bobby told me that everyone had stayed up all night, they were so excited to see us.

Before we could get to them we had to go through immigration. That meant trudging through a series of corrugated iron sheds, answering innumerable questions and being scrutinised by rather grumpy inspectors. Over 300 of us were herded like cattle and for a brief moment I wondered if we had been transported to another time and country. Was this Ellis Island a hundred years ago? We were no longer people, just a number. Depending on your number you were directed either to the signs for "Yungaba Immigration Centre and Hostel" or "Sponsored Immigrants." There were no welcome signs or even a kind smile from the officials.

What seemed like hours later we finally made it outside to the welcome hugs of the family, How five children, four adults and our luggage all fitted into my uncle's car is still a mystery but it did and we set off to their home about ten miles away. The drive itself was interesting along the Brisbane River, but as we came to the first bridge my heart sank. It looked like a giant child's Meccano set and it actually shook as we went across.

Further on over the bridge were rows of houses and shops with wooden awnings looking like a set from a Wild West movie. This was Woolloongabba. Nothing was taller than three stories with hardly a tree in sight. We slowed down after the bridge at some very large crossroads and came to a stop at flashing red lights and clanging bells. When a man waving a red flag walked across the centre of the crossroads with a freight train following behind, I was convinced more than ever that I was in an American movie and had begun to wonder what century I was in, let alone which country

Whilst we were stopped by the train my uncle waved towards the left where there were a couple of wooden stands and some large trees on a grassy mound and proudly told us that it was 'The Gabba' which meant nothing to us at all. Almost in hysterics by this time, all I could think of was – thank God they drive on the left side of the road.

After what seemed ages we finally arrived at my Aunt and Uncle's house, a three bedroom low wooden house in among rows of similar looking houses all with different coloured front doors. It reminded me of the song that went something like 'there's a pink one and a green one, and a blue one and a yellow one and they're all made of ticky tacky and they all look just the same.'

A couple of days later we drove to the nearest shopping area about 5 miles away. There were no large shopping centres then but little groups of shops, food, chemist, hardware, bakers, car sales etc. The main shop we went to was more like a warehouse. Everything was sold in bulk such as 10 pound bags of flour or 20 pound sacks of potatoes, carrots, onions and huge pumpkins I had never seen before. Of fruit there were only hands of bananas and bags of apples, no green vegetables. There were cases of tined goods and worst of all half pigs or sheep hanging up or enormous sides of beef, none of which I knew how to tackle. I burst into tears as we came out and all I could say to my husband was "I don't know how to feed you". Strain was beginning to tell after 48 hours in this strange country but this was only the beginning of our stint in paradise — paradise just got worse.

That first weekend passed in a blur of people coming and going and ending in a party on Sunday night with the local radio welcoming us to our new life down under. I went to bed with a nagging headache that was making me feel ill. On the Monday morning RJ had an interview in the city for a position in the local Government Office. All his qualifications had been sent from the UK Government and we had been assured they would place him in a Queensland government position when arrived. We had been told to inform them of our date of arrival and hence the letter for his interview was waiting when we arrived. He had been accepted for a position but with no indication of what position it would be.

The children and I sat on the steps of the lovely Victorian stone-built Treasury building soaking up the sunshine and watching the river flow by just a few hundred yards away. Traffic and people swirled around us and green clanking trams lumbered down the main street. Twenty minutes later RJ came out of the building looking as white as a ghost.

"What on earth is the matter?" I said looking at his distraught face. "I haven't got a job" he said "They have just told me I am two years too old" – he was then 30 years old.

Words were inadequate – horror was etched on both our faces. At that moment all I wanted to do was go home. There we were in a strange land with no job, very little money, two children, four suitcases and miles from anywhere. I'd already had enough in four days of Australia, and knew that however welcome we were in my Aunt's house we couldn't stay long. On top of that my headache was getting worse.

Tuesday morning found me unable to get out of bed. I was in agony and couldn't move my head at all. A few hours later found me in hospital in the city suffering from some tropical malaise that didn't seem to have a name but they thought I had picked up in Egypt. I didn't care where it came from as long as it could be cured. Every evening my Uncle and RJ visited me travelling over an hour each way. Children were not allowed. Ten days later I was able to leave hospital with a warning not to do anything energetic or it might come back. I never knew what it was.

A few weeks later we moved ourselves into a little ground floor flat near the centre of the city. It was a rather dilapidated flat in a three-storey wooden building. Having been empty for a while, the wildlife of fleas, cockroaches, mice and spiders had made it their home. Not to put too fine a point on it, we really didn't want to live in it but we had no choice at that time. Drastic fumigation was the order of the day. It took two days to rid the flat of wildlife and weeks for the smell to go away, but at least we had our own front door.

RJ had found a job in a supermarket. He had been a manager for a large chain of stores in the U.K. before moving to a government job and we had bought a little second (or sixth) hand VW car. My son of six had to go to school a few miles away and as I didn't drive he had to go by tram. This meant a walk up and down a very steep hill twice a day. It wasn't too bad in the morning heat, but the afternoon walk up and down the hill with the temperatures in the 90s, a fractious toddler, and the relentless sun beating down became sheer torture. I was frightened every day whether my little boy would get there and back safely and worried what I would do if he missed the tram. Mobile phones were a long way in the future.

I noticed each morning on my walk that the road was wet in the gutters, although there had been no rain. I mentioned this to my neighbour on the top floor flat and remarked how clean the streets were being kept. In a rather clipped English voice she remarked that no one cleaned the streets it was all the water from baths and sinks emptying along the road.

Trying not to show my horror I smiled and asked what part of England she was from.

"I'm Australian not English and I come from South Australia," and with that she shut the door in my face and hardly ever spoke to me again in the six months we were there.

The idea that English or British people were welcome in Australia was not strictly true. It had never occurred to me that we wouldn't be welcome. Didn't the Australian Government and Immigration people constantly tell us how welcome we would be and how they needed us to 'populate' Australia and build a lovely country together? Had no one told the Australians this was what was going to happen – it seems not. That was my first brush with discrimination towards the new immigrants, but worse was to come.

Distances between places were vast and I very quickly realised that I had to learn to drive a car – it was a necessity not a luxury. Public transport was very limited and it took almost two hours on a tram and two buses to reach my Aunt's house.

I had an ex-racing driver as a teacher who at the end of my lesson would say "you just steer and I'll press the pedals." A rather unorthodox way of learning to drive but we would zoom around the beautiful old parts of the City with their large white colonial style houses and roads lined with the beautiful blue blossoming Jacaranda trees. He did insist I drove in the City at the busiest times, coping with buses, trams and pedestrians as well as around the old twisty narrow and hilly back ways of the old parts of the City.

He was brilliant. I passed my test just before Christmas. Not only could I now drive our little VW to ferry the children around but I had also seen some of the beautiful picturesque parts of old Brisbane which beckoned me to explore one day. Many of the old white colonial houses had beautiful ironwork on gates, balconies and on gables underneath the roof. They were known as 'Iron Lace' and that described them beautifully.

Learning to drive had opened up a part of the City I had now come to live in. Many years later I came to dread the blossoming of the Jacaranda trees around the beautiful old Queensland houses, not because I didn't like them, but because it heralded exam time!

School and university terms commenced in February and ended in November so December and January, the hottest part of the year, were when most people took holidays.

That first Christmas holiday we managed to rent a little wooden cottage near a beach 70 miles north up the coast from Brisbane City. To us it was a long way to go but we soon found out that this was nothing in Australia, and certainly not when a few years later we were posted out to Western Queensland 820 miles from the City.

My daughter never ceased her chatter as we left Brisbane behind us on our first real outing. "Look Mum, camels!" I was all ready to say don't be silly when off towards some hill there appeared a string of about 20 camels. A few minutes later it was horses and then elephants. By this time I was growing tired of my child's interest in animals and I did say, "No darling there are no elephants here, Australia doesn't have elephants" but there, in a field, were four elephants! – It happened to be a travelling circus.

One animal we didn't see was a kangaroo although we had imagined they hopped all over the place (well, not down the main street). We finally made it to the cottage as the sun was going down and the cicadas began their deafening chorus. Immediately we arrived my daughter demanded the toilet so we rushed into the bathroom only to find no toilet, only a small bath and hand basin. A shed a good few yards down the narrow concrete path revealed a chemical toilet. Not quite what we expected but never mind.

The sun goes down rapidly in the sub tropics and by the time we had eaten and settled the children it was pitch black, no street lights. Only a few distant house lights broke the darkness. We felt very isolated. There were no lights inside or outside the toilet and when we opened the back door the light from inside showed the concrete path was full of frogs croaking in tune with the cicadas. We may have been isolated but it certainly wasn't quiet. RJ used a broom to sweep the frogs away and we never gave spiders a thought until the next day.

At 7am the next morning there was a knock on the door and our neighbour across the road wanted to know if we were all right. He was most helpful in showing us the spiders in the toilet and around the outside walls. These were Red Backs and highly dangerous along with the Cane Toads in the garden that could spit poison. "The Geckos and tree frogs are OK and you might see the odd Blue Tongue Lizard or Guano (short for Iguana) around but apart from that I'm sure you will be fine" and with that he went and we hadn't even had breakfast. We sprayed for the Red Backs and watched for the other wildlife. We got used to the little bright green Tree Frogs that would attach themselves at night to the windowpane outside. We were the ones in the goldfish bowl.

On our first venture to the beach we happily put up an umbrella, smothered ourselves in the recommended sunscreen cream, unpacked the picnic and settled on our first Australian golden beach. So, this was what we had come 12 thousand miles for – sun, sea and sand.

An hour later we were heading off the beach, my daughter crying and itching and me looking like a cooked lobster. It wasn't the sun, so the chemist said, but a reaction to the Government recommended sunscreen that we had used so liberally. After that if we went out at all we had to be completely covered up and in 35 degree heat it was no fun. The nights were hot and humid and I longed for some cool breeze to waft around me instead of mosquitoes, flying ants and Christmas beetles. We were not sorry when our week came to an end and we went back to have Christmas day with my family.

After our sojourn in the flat we managed to rent one of the houses near my Aunt. Indeed we could hop over the fence to her house. Her friends and neighbours rallied round to help us out with furniture until we could get on our feet. Nearly everyone around us was English or Scottish and swapping stories of why we had all emigrated passed many hours over a cup of tea or 'tinnies' (beer) for the men. Barbecues were just as we had been told to expect, men to one side and women to the other.

Happiness and sadness went hand in hand with trying to settle into a new land with its unpronounceable place names, heat, dust, flies and strange insects. That first summer left me exhausted just trying to cope with everything. I used to watch for the postman and hope for a letter from home. We had no phone. Money was very tight but we didn't starve. Our second Christmas was one I would like to forget with both children sick, RJ having to travel to the other side of the City and working long hours. We did manage Christmas stockings for the children and I made preserves for Christmas presents.

We needed extra money if we were going to survive. Trying to find myself a job was not easy. Most interviews were not to find out what I knew but rather to tell me that 'as you have two children and a husband you should be at home looking after them.' One interviewer abused me for coming over to Australia and expecting to get a job especially as I was 'B...' English. He shouted the last two words at me as I went out of the door.

Listening to other emigrants this was not an uncommon attack on women. Indeed, in many places, such as public services, police, banks etc., when a woman was getting married, she had to leave her job, so many jobs that were available in England to married women were closed in Australia.

The housing estate we lived on had been built alongside a large complex of factories from cars to plastics. Most of the neighbours around us worked in the factories and the British men had to constantly stand up for themselves. The Australian men didn't like the British coming in to take their jobs. Tension often ran high and even resorted to the odd fight, but slowly the Australians accepted them when they stood up for themselves.

My daughter was now at a nursery school but the hours I could work were limited. I took on night duty at the weekends in a Catholic Hospice in the old part of the city so that RJ could look after the children. Few of these older places had fly screens on the windows and were open to any of the flying insects such as cockroaches and beetles attracted by the lights. People who worked there seemed to take this for granted but I hated seeing the large brown flying cockroaches waving their antenna at you when you opened a drawer or cupboard, brown beetles running away when you turned the light on in the stock room and noises that were strange. I used to come home in the morning and scrub myself and my hair from top to bottom being frightened that I might bring something back to the children. Three months later I walked straight out of the door when one night I turned back the bedclothes of a very elderly and dying lady, to find half a dozen red flying cockroaches eating her.

Things slowly improved. We had made friends. My Aunt and Uncle were a tremendous help and we had lots of lovely family days together with barbecues, laughter and love. With the little money we had, and a very low mortgage, we managed to buy a wooden house on stilts with four bedrooms as RJ's mother had decided to join us in Australia. I then went to work in a children's outpatients department of a large hospital and my Mother-in-law looked after the children when they came home from school.

Twelve months later we were beginning to settle down when RJ applied and landed a new job with 'Shell.' We were overjoyed with a decent wage for him at last after the initial training. The one problem was that we may be on the move again, this time with his mother, two children, one dog and two white mice.

I never minded moving. As a child we had moved many times with my father initially being in the Army. Within nine months we were on our way to New South Wales. RJ's mother didn't want to come with us and went to live with my Aunt. This was going to be a whole new chapter in our lives, in fact more than we knew.

Waratah
Flower.

Lyn Cook

Chapter IV
LIFE WITH 'SHELL'

Lismore was a lovely place to live, being then a small country town with a population of 20,000 (today it is 120,000). I made friends with another 'Shell' wife who lived across the road and often when the men were away we would collect the children from school and squash into her very old Ford car and drive to the beach at Byron Bay to have a swim and a picnic. There were only a few houses scattered along the little road leading to the beach with a couple of houses and a caravan almost on the sea shore. It was very peaceful in the week and stunningly beautiful. Visiting it a few years ago it is now a highly populated tourist attraction, and although the Bay is still beautiful, it has lost its charm.

Our small two-bedroom flat was halfway up a steep hill and overlooked most of the school playing fields and town. We backed onto an area of forest that went for a mile or so further up the hill.

Being close to the so-called 'wild life' we constantly had to watch out for snakes and Red Back spiders who liked our brickwork around our very small flat. My neighbour kindly pointed out a Red Back spider's web so I could identify one when I saw it. Nothing like the beautifully symmetrical webs we used to see in the British hedgerows. We had the odd snake that slithered through the back of our garden but never came near our flat.

We quickly accustomed ourselves to the lovely town and I seemed to spend most of the weekends ferrying children and husband to various activities. RJ was a qualified Football Referee and not only refereed the league games but also ran some children's football at the weekends. He was also a Scout Master. Sometimes he was called to Brisbane to referee the larger football league matches. That meant a round trip of over 200 miles so we used to camp out in my Aunt's caravan in her garden if they hadn't taken it anywhere.

The journey to and from Brisbane passed through many miles of sugar cane which was beautifully green until harvest time. The cane was then burnt to eliminate a cane beetle. They could make you very sick or even kill you. Seeing the cane burning was startling but well controlled so you knew it was safe. We have driven on roads where the cane was burning on both sides and it was pretty scary. Then came the smell. No, not the cane burning, but the sickly sweet, almost visceral smell of crushed sugar. A smell I thought at first was revolting, but strangely I came to like it over time.

The journey from Lismore to Brisbane also went through steep hills and winding roads that for some reason made me car-sick. I came to dread the trip but I recovered after a little while and it was always nice to see the family and RJ's Mum.

There were some lovely little villages in the hills and stunning views towards the sea. Some of the small farms had begun diversifying and used their arable land for growing coffee, Macadamia nuts and Waratah flowers. Alstonville was a lovely village, high up in the hills which usually had a pleasant afternoon sea breeze and would perhaps one day be a nice place for retirement.

To keep myself busy I decided to do a two year course at the technical college with dress designing, pattern making, home furnishings and fine needlework. This was the age of mini-skirts, hot-pants and long white boots. Being in collage we had all the latest fashions to hand and dressed accordingly.

Malcolm became a Cub and RJ did his football refereeing with both schools and League games in NSW and Brisbane's major league. Jane-Ann took up ballet dancing which she had a real aptitude for. I spent my weekends ferrying children and husband around football fields and halls. We loved being in Lismore and we were sorry when RJ had to take up a new territory.

Chapter V

THE REAL UNKNOWN

We had been in Lismore two years and our next posting was to a place called Longreach. Having no idea where that was I dashed across the road to look at a friend's large map. Happily I searched up and down the seacoast to no avail. 'Go up the coast to Rockhampton and then go inland' said my friend. I did this but couldn't find it. 'Turn the page' she said, grinning. There it was, a little dot on the map 460 miles inland – the real outback. I had no idea what to expect but I knew it was a long way from friends and family.

RJ had been flown up there for a few days to find some accommodation. When he returned he had found us a lovely house Queensland Style. It took us two days to drive the 820 miles from Brisbane to Longreach with two fractious children, two terrified white mice and a small Golden Retriever of five months old who wanted all of the back seat.

We stayed overnight in a motel and set off the next morning for the rest of the journey. It was overcast but not too hot. We had a small box in the passenger foot-well which was the air-conditioning. Whoever sat in that seat had to have a blanket around their legs as it was only one-directional therefore very cold for that person. We stopped somewhere for lunch but unbeknown to me my daughter had let out one of the mice. As we stopped it jumped out of her hands. She screamed not to get out as RJ had opened his door. He shut the door quickly and retrieved the mouse putting it back into its cage. Panic over. It was a long, long journey through scrubby flat dull land that didn't change except for the little hamlets we passed through every sixty or so miles.

The light was beginning to go as we neared the end of the journey. Ahead of us was another small group of about thirty houses either side of the road. I could just see the lights in the distance of one row of street lights. 'This is it' said RJ. I looked with horror at the few houses and one road and broke down in tears. 'I can't live here' I sobbed. The children remained quiet. RJ realised how upset I was and quickly assured me that he was only joking and we had another few miles to go to Longreach.

Making it to the one and only Motel was a real feat of endurance, and what a relief to be in some cool air. Next morning the weather was again overcast and therefore a little cooler as we left the Motel for our house, which I hadn't yet seen. RJ went and collected the keys and we waited for the removal vans that were coming from two different places as we had had most of our belongings in storage for two years whilst we were in New South Wales. I was pleasantly surprised by the house, built in brick in the old Queensland style with a high-pitched roof and deep verandas (no lovely 'Iron Lace') but no removal vans greeted us. The children and dog explored a very large back garden or 'The Yard' as the Queenslanders called any back area.

Our first removal van arrived an hour later with two rather tired looking removal men. All of us sat on the ground in the shade as the temperature began to climb and we waited for RJ to return with the keys. An hour later we were still there but eventually, by lunch time, RJ and the keys turned up, RJ muttering about the keys being lost, and we let ourselves into a very hot house. The reason for the delay was because no one much locked their doors, so no one knew where the keys were and the Agent had to send someone out 50 miles to the sheep farm to the man who owned the property.

Our first task was to sort out the three taps in the kitchen. One connected to the hot water tank but wasn't switched on, one came out with muddy coloured water and one didn't work at all. Nothing was drinkable to make a cup of tea. Our removal men got a little fed up and disappeared to the local pub. Three hours later a plumber arrived on the heels of the second lot of removal men. They announced that they were going meet their mates in the pub. We never saw them again that day, so in 12 hours we had ended up with two removal vans, four men who had disappeared, (I suspect rather tipsy) and who hadn't done anything except block our drive way and get the water connected, only to be told we couldn't drink it anyway as it was tank water which had been stagnant for years.

We all escaped back to the coolness and comfort of the Motel. It obviously wasn't going to be the usual kind of removal so we booked a few more nights in the beautifully air-conditiond Motel, just to be on the safe side.

The next day it was raining but thankfully a little cooler. We opened up the house and by midday everything was in the house or garage and the men set off for the eighteen-hour drive back to the city. Everything was suddenly deathly quiet. The children had fallen asleep on the settee; the dog laid spread-eagled like a frog in a small patch of shade and the perspiration streamed down our faces in the rising heat. The sun beat relentlessly on the tin roof and I longed for a cool bath, or even to go back to the City with the removal men.

The house had green wooden venetian blinds on the outside of the windows making it rather dark. I realised later how valuable they were in keeping the house a little cooler. I noticed that when the weather was hot many houses kept their windows firmly closed and curtains drawn until well into the day. I soon learnt to do the same as it helped to retain the cooler night temperature.

Air conditioning was well in the future for houses and fans were the only means to help keep cool, but by the time it was over 40 degrees all they did was push the hot air around. At the first opportunity we bought a portable machine called a 'Bonair,' which was a tank of water with a fan blowing over the top of the water. That was fine in the dry heat but when it became humid it was almost impossible to breathe.,

I managed to spin out staying in the Motel for another few days enabling us to unpack at our leisure in the house. Most of the first night in our house I spent listening to unfamiliar sounds. The roof continually cracked as the tin cooled down, the large trees at the bottom of the garden moaned in the slightest breeze and shuffling sounds on fly screens had me petrified that some unknown creature was trying to get in.

I was pleased to see daylight but looking at the clock it said 4.30 a.m. I groaned and turned over but to no avail. I soon learnt why everyone in the outback is up and doing by 5 o'clock in the morning because by 9 o'clock, if the housework etc has not been done, it's too hot after that to do very much. Of course one had to sometimes but I soon fell into the habit of waking up with the sunrise.

The second morning we were woken up at 6.30 a.m. with someone knocking on our screen door and our dog trying to jump through the mesh from our side of the door. It was the milkman who, when calm reigned, explained he came every day including Christmas day as the cows still produced milk and he had to deliver it. His herd of cattle grazed on the far side of the Thompson River to the town and only when the river flooded did we not have a delivery of fresh milk and cream.

It was most unusual to have a herd of milking cows in the outback. He sent most of his milk to Rockhampton 420 miles away to be bottled but he was allowed to have a Warm Milk licence to sell to the residents of the town. It was indeed straight from the cow and not pasteurised but was TT tested. Like our grandmothers before us he ladled the milk out from the churn into our large jug. It was lovely milk and the cream was even better. The dog never barked again at the milkman except one Christmas morning when it was raining and the milkman was wearing a hat – the dog didn't recognise him.

When we moved into the house I had noticed the bath was stained a grim shade of coffee and I did everything to get rid of it and have a bath. I finally ran the water and coming back a few minutes later found the water was rather more than light coffee-coloured – it was chocolate. River water, our friendly plumber told us. A filter helped solve some of the problem but from then on showers were the order of the day so I couldn't see the colour of the water. Just occasionally, when it was too hot to cope with, I would fill the bath up with cold water and sink gratefully into the brown water. If there was anything I wanted to keep white in the washing I had to use our tank water, which was now very precious and expensive to buy in if it didn't rain. We had had the tank cleaned and filled which was very expensive. Before we left we had proper town water installed. Even so the taste was not very nice but putting it in the fridge for twenty four hours made it drinkable. Needless to say by the time we left most white items were a faint brown.

It seemed no time at all before I was facing the long eighteen-hour coach journey taking my 12-year-old to school over 1,000 miles away. There was no air-conditioning or facilities on the coach. Not a prospect either of us relished but it was necessary. When we knew we were posted to Longreach we had to look at the schooling. There was only one high school that was very small and basic up to sixteen years only. We quickly decided that boarding school was the best option for our son. That at least meant that wherever we were posted the children's schooling would remain stable. We decided on a boarding school in Lismore where some of his friends would be going as day pupils, and it might help to see someone he knew. It wouldn't be long before our daughter would also be wending her way south to her school in the same New South Wales City of Lismore.

The trip was long and hot with a child of twelve who really didn't want to go to a boarding school for six years. After 18 hours to Brisbane we had to cross the city to another coach station for a further three-hour journey into NSW and a very tearful goodbye. The journey home he would have to do all on his own as there were only freight trains from Longreach to Brisbane, no passenger trains.

By the time I returned from NSW a few days later the weather was at its worst. Being so far from the coast and on the edge of the Simpson Desert it was usually a hot dry heat in the West but having broken an eight-year drought it continued to rain on and off and the humidity nearly went off the scale. For over two weeks the temperature never dropped below 100 degrees night or day. How on earth I was going to survive years here was a real question I asked myself.

I remember the day in the wickedly cold winter of 1963, when this had all begun, asking RJ if he could take us somewhere warm. Now I had my wish but didn't expect to be roasted alive. The awful hot weather ended in a spectacular storm. I was giving afternoon tea to a lady from church and her five-year-old daughter when it started to hail quite gently but sounded loud in the roof. The child fled behind my settee screaming, the dog set up a howl and the hail became heavier and heavier coupled with thunder and lightning. Eventually the storm lessened to rain, the dog disappeared under our bed and we managed to quieten the little girl who continued to cling to her mother's skirt but wouldn't go outside the door to go home. It was still raining with the ground covered with inches of hail-stones. It turned out that they had been living even further west than we were and had only just arrived in Longreach. In her short life of five years the little girl had never seen rain or hailstones.

Later on when I set up the primary school library and came to know the children I discovered very many of them had no concept of the sea or any building higher than three stories. Pictures were just that, and trying to explain how large and salty the sea was, or going up in a lift thirty floors was like describing something from outer-space.

Life in the outback was very different from anything I had been used to. Apart from anything else, RJ was away three or four days in the week, and my daughter and I had to fend for ourselves. There was no television and only one ABC radio channel and a local town channel. I was so bored and hot the first few weeks, but also recovering from a bout in hospital just before we moved, that I couldn't summon up enough energy to do anything. Those first few weeks I had only taken my daughter to school, attended school and shopped a few times in the one and only main street.

Houses were set far apart and the next door house was empty. On the other side was an elderly lady who never left the house. Our road was wide with a large central strip of scrubby grass and trees so one couldn't see much of the houses across the road. Eventually, one Sunday afternoon RJ urged me to go to an Arts

Council meeting just a few houses up the road. I was tired and hot and hated the place but I couldn't sit and moan, so I went. The first person I saw was a lady from church who introduced me and made me welcome. I came back carrying the secretary's folder and wondering what I had let myself in for. I certainly wasn't going to be bored now!

By this time we had been in Australia nearly seven years and I had not seen my parents since we left. When we sailed in 1965 we really had no expectations of when or if we would return to the UK. With one child at boarding school and one at home RJ suggested that if I could find a little job I could save up to visit my parents at the end of our three years. Having just having finished a dress design/fine needlework course in Lismore I really couldn't see much use for it in outback Queensland, but perhaps there were other jobs I could find.

RJ was a member of the Rotary Club and asked around for me. Three weeks later I found myself behind a counter of the local Totaliser (government run betting shop) taking bets on Saturday morning. A far cry from needlework, but fun as I had never been in a betting shop in my life. I wondered if it was my very modern mini skirt or swinging culottes that helped me get the job and not my husband's Rotary pals. Just coming from college I was wearing all the trendy outfits, most of them very skimpy – just right for the hot weather I thought until my daughter came home one day crying. I finally managed to find the cause of the tears. "It's not me it's you Mummy, your clothes are all funny and I get laughed at when you walk to school with me."

Obviously the end of my Hot Pants and mini skirt era!

Chapter VI
LIFE IN THE WEST

One of the things I found hard was the sheer isolation. The nearest place was sixty miles away and exactly like the place we lived in, a few houses, petrol station, some shops, Stock and Station offices, Council Hall, small school and a betting shop. The heat, flies and dusty brown landscape with a metallic blue sky overhead was no different to any other place within hundreds of miles, so unless one was going to these places for a specific reason there was little point in going anywhere. All these small places had become quite self-sufficient and I wondered why they were fifty or sixty miles apart. I eventually found that they had originally been staging posts for the Cobb & Co transport and postal service, and fifty to sixty miles was as far as the horses could go in one day. They were in fact staging posts for changing the horses. The City of

Brisbane was eight hundred and twenty miles away, so post was a little slower then!

The first few weeks of relentless heat that sapped one's energy to do anything after 9 a.m. was quite frightening. How could I last three years of insects, heat, flies, boredom (now sorted) and isolation? The answer was to do something and forget the heat. I soon learnt to have the house sprayed regularly for insects – spiders and geckos were immune! – inspect shoes before putting them on, have all dried food tightly sealed, never leave any food uncovered and try to ignore the flying insects like large brown cockroaches, stink beetles, moths, sand flies and other unknown wildlife that constantly pounded the fly-screens at night. It was a great relief when the weather finally cooled down to a pleasant 3 or 4 degrees in the morning to 25 degrees in the middle of the day. We were on the edge of the Simpson Desert so these widely fluctuating temperatures were to be expected – except by me.

I threw myself into country life and found a wealth of activities from a theatre group to tennis. The Australian Arts Council was very sympathetic in the 1970s to the needs of the people far out from towns and cities. We had many visiting musicians, actors, artists, potters, and overseas travelling companies, but more of the Arts Council later. Our pleasure in the cooler weather in the winter would be to drive 120 miles on a Sunday afternoon to a large Station (Sheep Station of over 10,000 acres) for a couple of games of tennis, a cup of tea and drive home. There was also a small tennis group in town where they actually had a grass court. It was a real pleasure to play on grass.

Although insects were the bane of my life in the summer surprisingly we saw very few snakes – but lots of other insects. I must say I refrained from exploring the overgrown and abandoned chicken sheds at the far end of our property. Even the dog gave them a wide berth as her long coat always picked up burrs and ticks. I became very adept at removing ticks before they could do much damage because they could make an animal, or human, very sick and even kill a child. Snakes were however to be part of my life while we were there.

Someone I met at the theatre group also collected snakes for the Brisbane Museum on a regular basis and would ring me up to hold the snakes so he could do a scale count which would tell the age of the snake. Some snakes were very rare and highly poisonous. One Sunday morning rather early, I found myself agreeing on the phone to go and hold a small snake for a scale count. The snake was gently anaesthetised and handed to me; it was no longer than seven or eight inches and held no fear for me. Unfortunately that snake did not recover from the anaesthetic. We could only use a simple cone with Ether dropped on it and it was therefore difficult to estimate the strength of the Ether. The second snake was not quite so anaesthetised and we did the scale count safely and put it in its box ready for transport to the Museum.

"I will tell you now" said my friend "these snakes are some of the most venomous snakes that have come from New Guinea and have never been seen so far south in Queensland." My mouth went very dry but I was safe; they had looked like harmless little yellow striped grass snakes to me. I was very glad I didn't know what they were before I agreed to hold them.

In his house my friend had quite a few carpet snakes that lived in very large glass tanks and fed on live mice. My daughter was very upset when she realised he was breeding white mice for the snakes' breakfasts, especially as she had two at home as pets. She wasn't particularly frightened of the snakes but didn't like them out of the tank. However, most very young children are not frightened of snakes and sometimes we would take some of the small carpet snakes to the Kindergarten – with of course prior arrangement with the teacher. She shut herself away whilst we were there –

she was absolutely terrified of snakes but the children couldn't get enough of them.

One was always watchful for snakes but on the whole they would rather go away from you unless you startled them, but children in the outback were taught to respect them. One morning when I glanced out of the library window in the school where I was working I saw a large brown snake wriggling very slowly across the playground between two wings of the school. It was only ten minutes before lunch when a couple of hundred noisy children would come pouring onto the playground. I flew to the Headmaster for help to find someone to catch the snake and delay the ringing of the bell that could also send the snake into hiding. We found the caretaker just in time. I watched as he came up behind the snake, caught it in a cleft stick, picked it up by its tail and cracked it like a whip breaking its back and killing it. He then dropped it into the incinerator. The whole episode lasted less than five minutes. It was sad for the snake but as the most venomous snake in Australia it had to be done to protect the children.

Sentiment plays little part in the country when there are literally life and death situations to be weighed up. Animals in the outback fall into three groups: working animals such as dogs and horses; food that is mostly sheep or cattle and wildlife such as rabbits, wild pigs, emus and kangaroos. The children learn this lesson from a very young age as for many of them the land will be their future.

My daughter missed her ballet classes as there was nothing in Longreach but one day she asked if she could play the piano. Where this came from I don't know but there was always music in our house. I had played the piano until I was married but we had no room for my piano and I hadn't played for many years. We advertised for a piano and found a very nice upright one but woefully out of tune. In fact it had never been tuned in its life. Where could one find a piano tuner and someone to give Jane-

Ann some lessons? Advertising brought nothing. The only place I knew where some music was taught was the catholic school. I was told they didn't take outsiders.

Well, I had nothing to lose by asking myself. I made an appointment with the head of the Convent and school and went to talk to her. We had a nice long chat about England and Ireland and little about music. Eventually she agreed to send the piano tuner to our house when he came next although she couldn't guarantee he would be able to fit me in but she would ask. He only came once or twice a year from Rockhampton. She agreed to take Jane-Ann for lessons when the piano had been tuned. It did all work out and Jane-Ann was the only non catholic music student. I think it also helped that I could sing descant and later sang at some of their services. Jane-Ann went on to study piano at the Brisbane Conservatorium.

The first summer slowly came to an end and with it the change in the clock from summertime. It was in fact the first and last time Queensland put their clocks forward one hour for the summer and for the people in the outback it was terrible. It wasn't so much that the sun didn't go down until nearly 9 p.m. but nor did the heat, meaning that late into the night the temperature was often over 100 degrees. Eating dinner late or trying to get children to sleep in the heat was a real trial. The school tried opening at eight o'clock but by two o'clock the children were tired, with the smaller ones falling asleep. This wasn't working for us in the outback. Luckily The Queensland Government listened to the country people and it was never done again. The cooler weather was a blessed relief when the season changed.

Chapter VII

ARTS COUNCIL

Now, as I mentioned, I had volunteered as the local secretary for the Arts Council. I was determined to do my best for the expanding Arts Council and encourage as many people as possible to attend the shows, from dancing to opera. I had never done anything like this before, so it was all a new experience. I would certainly learn on the job.

Longreach was a town that had many 'itinerants' over the last few years. It was the original home of QANTAS and still had a small airport. It was also a centre for three banks, stock and station agents and oil companies, (BP and Shell) so there was a small constantly shifting population. These 'itinerants' were not always liked by the permanent residents. Many of the outlying stations (farms) had been hit hard with the eight-year drought that had just broken, but it had meant that men had been laid off and the women of the house had stepped in. Many women in the outback had therefore no time, or energy, for socialising. The Arts Council programme of theatre, art, music or drama was a long way from being part of their lives.

Longreach had a large primary school, a small Catholic primary school, a high school that only taught pupils up to 16 years and a fairly new Agricultural College. As I had begun work in the primary school, I had lots of contact with the children and parents, but not with the people in the High School, Catholic School or Agricultural College.

One of my first Arts Council shows was just a few weeks after I had taken over. The previous secretary had returned to Canberra, so I was in at the deep end. Posters and tickets had arrived. Now what do I do?

I took myself off to the local radio station and introduced myself. We realised we had met a few weeks before at one of the tennis Sunday afternoons. Next minute I was on-air! The range of the airway covered the town with about a 50 mile radius. Next I visited the Schools and College offering two free tickets in each place. I then walked the length of the main street, Eagle Street, and asked every shop to put up a poster. The Lebanese Restaurant/ Coffee shop agreed to sell the tickets as I tackled their strong sweet Turkish coffee which I came to love.

This first show was an indoor dance and acrobatic extravaganza with penny-farthing bikes. On the day itself I had penny-farthing bikes being ridden up and down the high street and clowns saying 'G'day' popping in and out of the shops. We even took two penny-farthing bikes and riders to the primary school during their lunch break. I'm pleased to say we had a very full house for my first Arts Council venture.

It was always fun when a visiting Arts Council group came and one day it was the 'Black Theatre of Prague' We had arranged a welcome lunch for them and just one hour before I met them from that little nine-seater plane I was asked if we had a Czech or German speaking interpreter as they spoke very little English. – This was rural, isolated country, not the city!

I dashed down to the local radio station and asked if they could put this over the radio, offering a free lunch to anyone speaking those languages if they would act as an interpreter for a couple of hours. The radio station had a reply within minutes. One gentleman turned up at the hotel restaurant. It was our pest control man who had sorted out my house just a few weeks before. We had a pleasant lunch and I deposited the theatre group back to the Motel and looked forward to a couple of hours rest – not to be. Two large suitcases were left in the car, which, I gathered by hand gestures, they would like ironed for the evening's performance.

In over 40-degree heat I donned my coolest scrap of clothing and set to work. Most of their wardrobe consisted of skirts and blouses but there were also some of the most beautiful scarves and pashminas of silk that I had seen. (Pashminas were originally made from fine goat's wool.) Unfortunately most of them were in a dreadful state and I spent most of the afternoon doing my best to repair them.

The performance was a great success and the next morning they put on a special dance performance for the schools. We had a full hall. One rather large, smiling and bearded guitar player had all the children enthralled with tricks as well as the guitar playing. He was really the only one that spoke to us. The rest of the troop did not talk but smiled and danced.

We knew someone in the dance troupe was the Commissar who reported back to the secret police and we tried to work out who it might be. It had to be someone who understood English but none of them let on, hence the need for an interpreter. This was the 1970s when there were quite a few defectors from the Communist

Countries such as Nureyev from Russia. Australia was seen as a good place to ask for political asylum. I found out later that our smiling guitar playing man was the Commissar and the husband and wife ballet dancers in the troop did in fact speak English, and tried to defect when they reached Sydney. I'm not sure if they ever made it.

Only six weeks after my first Arts Council show was an Opera Group. How would Opera go down in the outback I wondered? I gathered it was the first time 'Opera' had been sent to the outback. Two gentleman and three ladies arrived in a large but battered van containing themselves and all the props. It was just after Christmas and the weather was very hot and unusually humid with threatening rainclouds. Electric storms had raged across the desert for nights but not yet turned into rain. Interestingly none of them had been over the mountain range and into the outback. Neither had they any idea how long it would take or what a single track road was like in black soil. They were to find out the hard way.

Luckily I found out their programme in advance and it was mostly excerpts from opera and ending with some Gilbert & Sullivan. Once again my trusty DJ advertised the programme a good few days before by playing some of the soundtracks from the operas and G&S. We had quite a good audience and were amazed when over a dozen students from the College turned up at the door. The Rotary and Lions Clubs were always good supporters and the G&S choruses had to be repeated with great applause and laughter. Again I had bombarded the shops with posters and a big write-up and advertisement in the local paper that came out once a week. It took some persuading for them to accept a write-up but they would if we gave them a paid advert. (My first bit of real writing. Little did I know that I would one day earn money from my writing.)

The next day the opera group was off to Winton, another

178 km (about 112 miles) northwest but mostly on dirt tracks, no more single track tarmac roads. We waved them good bye at ten in the morning. About two in the afternoon a plea came on the radio for a tractor to pull out a van on the Winton Road that was stuck in black soil. I just knew in my heart it was my Arts Council singers, and it was. At five o'clock a very dirty van and five weary people arrived at my door. I had by then arranged for four of them to sleep at one of the pubs as the Motel was full, and one stay with me. I had cooked a large spaghetti bolognese and big fruit salad. Luckily RJ was at home and his job was the bar. He made a very good 'Mine Host'. We all sat around after dinner and had our own impromptu concert. As I could sing I managed to join in.

It rained that night and in the morning it was still lashing down. We hadn't had rain for months and before long all the roads out of Longreach were impassable with the main Thompson and Barcoo rivers rising rapidly. Two days later the rain stopped but no one could go anywhere except by plane. Henry had to stay behind ready to drive the van to Brisbane when the road south was open again. The other four singers were flown home and the rest of the tour had to be cancelled. Henry stayed with us until the roads were passable. He came a few times to Longreach and always managed to spend time with us. His company was fun and with food, wine and music we had many happy evenings. We had a nice opera collection but he especially loved Benjamin Britten. I didn't have any of Britten's operas but luckily I had bought the War Requiem just before we left Lismore.

Henry Howell was not only the lead tenor but scene mover, administrator and driver. Everyone had to wade in and do everything, as well as sing. Just after his last trip to us Henry said he was going to England, where he was born, to further his studies. He became a leading tenor in the English National Opera and sang oratorio all around Europe.

Ten years later he returned to Australia so that his daughter of five years old could meet her maternal grandparents for the first time. The little one was to undergo a serious heart operation and it could go either way. Henry came for six months as 'Artist in Residence' to the college I worked in. We had lost contact in those years and it was such a surprise when he saw me. He had just given a G and S concert with students in our College theatre and I went to see it. I was just walking down the wide staircase when his loud voice called out my name. It felt like the whole college turned and looked at me. It was quite a moment, pleasure and embarrassment at the same time.

A few years later he became my singing teacher in the 1990s when I auditioned for the Brisbane Conservatorium. His friendship lasted until he died a few years after we came back to live in England in 1996. He loved the newspaper the Evening Standard and when I visited London I always bought a copy and sent it to him. Apparently it was also passed on to another friend of his from London so it was a well-travelled and read newspaper.

The Arts Council had a strong influence in the outback in the 1970s realising how isolated we were from mainstream arts and did their best to encourage and support activities. In Longreach there was a thriving group of spinners and weavers (we were after all surrounded by thousands of sheep!) and a large pottery group that rented a dilapidated old cottage a few doors away and they kindly let my daughter spend many happy hours with them. I still have the little slab pottery pot she made aged ten.

There had been an art group but it had disbanded. The Arts Council came up with the idea of sending out a visiting artist and lined up Mr Mervin Moriarty to fly his own plane to three outback towns including Longreach. He would come three or four times a year if I could reorganise the art group. We could have our own 'Flying Artist.' Once again my trusty DJ put out a call for local artists. The first time 'Merv' flew in it was during a rain storm but thankfully not a lot of wind. We tied down his little two-seater plane and headed for our gathering of a dozen people. It was a happy gathering as four of the group already knew Merv from his visit a year or so ago to assess if such a scheme would work. By the end of the meeting nine of us signed up to do a two-year distance learning art course and organise an afternoon children's class (with permission from the Primary School Headmaster).

Through the Arts Council we had a wonderful two years of art and art history as well as visits from some well-known professional artists such as Irene Amos and Robert Forster (Potter) who ran a school for us once a year. These week-long schools were very popular with local artists, potters and weavers. It was held in the large sheep-shearing sheds in the local show ground and we always ended with lots of laughter, wine and the obligatory barbecue.

Chapter VIII
FIRST ESCAPE

The end of the first year saw our first escape from the outback. All Shell personnel and wives were summoned to Brisbane – the men for a two-day conference and ladies for a chance to hit the shops or visit family. It ended with a dinner, speeches and dancing. The hotel was new and modern with swimming pool. spa, gym and restaurants built next to the Brisbane River and surrounded by the beautiful blue Jacaranda trees which were all in full bloom that year. However, we had to get there first.

Leaving the outback was by road or plane (a passenger train only ran once or twice a week to Rockhampton and none to Brisbane). We went by plane. It was very hot and unusually humid that December and a ground mist lay heavily across the airfield early that morning. It was a small nine-seater single-engine plane that was almost lost in the mist. Our pilot assured us he knew the runway, even in the mist. I wasn't very happy about such a small plane in the first place but was determined to get away, so I took a deep breath and strapped myself in behind the pilot.

We could not go above ten thousand feet because we were not pressurised and it made for a bumpy ride. As the day heated up, the rising air currents from the land buffeted the plane. I was pleased to see our first landing strip coming up in Alfa. We were just a matter of feet from the tarmac when a kangaroo jumped out of the bush directly into our path. The pilot reacted quickly, lifting the plane sharply away from the ground and throwing us back into our seats. The scream of the little engine and sudden lift left us all a little shaken. We went round again and landed safely a few minutes later. It was a relief to get out for a few minutes.

We were in the clouds about ten minutes away from landing at the large international airport of Rockhampton when the pilot was told to alter course as an international jet plane was coming in on the same trajectory as we were, but didn't know how far above us it was. At this stage we were still in patchy cloud and the pilot stood up and looked around all the windows. Where was the other plane? As we began to descend we were directed to a small side grass runway and could see a small plane like ours just in front of us. We landed a couple of minutes behind it. We had no sooner touched down when the jet roared above us landing on the major runway. The pilot looked rather shocked and I felt very sick. Perhaps I shouldn't have been behind the pilot. We managed to make it into the terminal where some friends were also waiting and they quickly took me to the ladies rest-room and my breakfast landed in the sink. I was not looking forward to the next part of the journey but it was at least a 747. I was never more relieved to land in Brisbane and find a comfortable bed in our hotel.

The next day we had free until six o'clock for the speeches and dinner. With posh dresses, glittering jewellery and some lovely cold wine we partied until midnight. Our table, for some reason I don't remember, had been awarded some special wine. Even with the air-conditioning it was hot and we all managed to drink the wine like lemonade. I was not feeling like breakfast the next morning. RJ said I persuaded the whole coach to sing on the way back to our hotel and I conducted them. Well......

The men went to their last morning conference whilst the ladies were taken to a brand new shopping centre which was then the largest one in Australia. A final afternoon tea was almost the end of our stay. Only those of us that had flights home the next day stayed on. That evening we had a lovely quiet walk along the river. I'm not sure either of us relished more years in the outback but we knew we were not there for ever. I must say the journey home was uneventful and we flew in a much larger plane directly from Brisbane to Longreach.

Malcolm came home a few days later for eight weeks and we had our first Christmas together in the outback.

Locust.
Lynn Cooke.

Chapter IX
PLAGUES, DEBUTANTES AND A BISHOP

We had three plagues in our second year – mice, locusts and stink beetles. Mice plagues are a strange phenomenon. They breed in their thousands and then millions and then begin swarming, eating anything to stay alive, from crops, rubber, insulation, textiles, plaster, inside cars and even animals. There had been a heavy drought in Queensland for eight years until 1971 so when the drought broke the conditions were right. This plague in 1972 began in the Northern Territory and swarmed south. They like humid damp weather but cold and heavy rainfall will wipe them out. They all died about a hundred miles from us when they hit dry arid land with nothing for them to eat. They died within two days so they never reached us but it was frightening.

The locusts (look like grasshoppers) on the other hand did

reach us, horrifying swarms of black swirling insects up to 45mm long. They came in waves for days, eating anything they landed on. RJ had to drive through them and the smell was rank as they hit the car radiator grill and cooked. It lasted about a week. In the middle of this RJ was away so there was just me and Jane-Ann in the house. Somehow, one night some managed to get into the house attracted by the lights. Screaming in her bedroom at these flying clicking insects I put her in Malcolm's room where there were no lights, sprayed her room and got rid of them. Although still crying, I put her back to bed with the door shut for now until I could rid the house of them.

To my dismay I realised the outside front door light was attracting them. The switch was also outside the door. I had to turn it off. I was as frightened as my daughter but there was no one else to help, I just had to kill the light. The fly screen door banged shut behind me as I stepped outside and steeled myself to turn off the light as they buzzed around me. As I turned back, the fly screen door was a black moving clicking, buzzing mass and I had to put my hand through them to open the door. I froze, all I could think of was that I had a crying child inside, I had to get in. The back door was locked so this was the only way in. I was physically sick when I made it through the door. I managed to kill those that had made it in with me. Jane-Ann finally fell asleep in my bed with me. I'm not sure who was the more frightened that night.

In November 1973 we decided to drive to Rockhampton to stay in a friend's house whilst they went to Brisbane to visit her parents. The 427 mile trip was uneventful and we arrived to wave off our friends and look after their two Burmese cats. Our first week was lovely and we had many beach trips and a bit of real shopping. The second week it began to rain and didn't let up. Rain and a cyclone lashed the coast and the rivers began to rise quickly. Our friends in Brisbane decided to make a dash for home before they were cut off and couldn't get back. They were almost the last over the Fitzroy Bridge in Rockhampton before it was closed. We made frantic attempts to book a train home both for the car, us and a large dog. Roads were impassable, as all roads to the West were cut.

Now there were four adults, four children, two cats and our Golden Retriever in a three-bedroom house. The house was on stilts and we had over a foot of water under the house. One didn't go outside without Wellington boots as the wildlife was trying to find a dry place. Snakes were not uncommon in the water and our Golden Retriever was not too fond of water either!

RJ had to get back to Longreach and was able to get a seat on the first train out. I then had to drive the car to the train loading yard and wait in a queue to load the car and then get tickets on a passenger train for me the children and the dog. I queued for two days and nights in the yard to load the car. Our friends looked after the children and dog. They took it in turns to change places with me so I could go and have a shower etc. The car was finally on the train but the sleeper passenger train was only going two days later.

This was my first train journey in Australia. Luckily my friends knew that this was a pre-war non air-conditioned train with no restaurant car. We did have our own separate compartment with a drop-down bunk but nothing else. By the time we finally made it to the train my friends settled the children in the carriage with water, food, blankets and pillows, whilst I had to lock the dog in an outside cage at the front of the train just behind the engine. I had just got back onto the train when it began to move. By the time I reached our carriage I had two very frightened and tearful children who thought I had missed the train.

When it stopped at the little stations one could buy food snd drink. Luckily we were well-provisioned including some books and games for the children. We had no idea how long the trip would take to reach Longreach as at least a dozen large creeks were rising and there were rockfalls on the track over the Bogunturgan Range and Kanoloo Black Mountains since the last passenger train had gone through. We were often stopped for hours and some passengers even helped to clear the track just outside the town of Bogantungan. The speed was sometimes about four miles an hour at walking pace over the mountains. Every time we stopped officially I had to take the dog out of the cage and give it a little walk and water. She became more and more frightened and I wondered if I would still have a dog at the end of this trip. It was a nightmare trip for all of us. Our train was the last one out of Rockhampton for a few weeks. Four days later, I was never more pleased to see the sign of 'Welcome to Longreach. Gateway to the Outback,' and a smiling RJ waiting with the car.

In January 1974, our third year in Longreach, our daughter was off to Lismore in NSW with her brother. She was going to the girls' boarding school. She was just so excited it was hard to keep her calm. She kept looking at her new school uniform and adding things to her new suitcases. For some reason Malcolm had to return to school a week before Jane-Ann so she would be travelling on her own. She had come with us when we went to pick Malcolm up at the end of term so hopefully she would know the way.

Malcolm had no sooner reached school when we had another massive cyclone hit Queensland. It rained for days even reaching us. The rivers rose and high tides hit the coast with the cyclone destroying properties all along the coast. Jane-Ann had to wait a week before setting off. The day came and we waved her off with the coach driver we had got to know very well. We knew he would look after her and see her across the city to the next coach.

They reached Barcaldine and the coach driver phoned us to say the river 'Alice' (Barcoo River tributary) was up and they couldn't cross the bridge as it was unsafe. There was a coach coming from

Brisbane and they had managed to find some boats to ferry the passengers and luggage across but couldn't do that until the other coach arrived and that wouldn't be until the next day. There were only six passengers going south and they decided to stay on the coach. Obviously Jane-Ann couldn't so what did we want to do? RJ phoned the Motel where he was known, having stayed there many times. Could they look after a twelve-year-old?

We phoned back to the coach driver waiting in the garage and then talked to Jane-Ann. Did she want us to come and bring her back or stay in the Motel? She elected to stay but we made sure she understood we would come and get her if she changed he mind. A couple of hours later the Motel owner phoned to say she was fine and had dinner with them and was helping with the washing up.

Somewhere near midnight the phone rang with a tearful daughter – she wasn't sure she wanted to stay. I was all for jumping in the car but by the time we reached her it would be morning. We talked her to sleep.

The next morning she was fine and apparently had happily helped to take the breakfasts to the other Motel guests. Soon after the Motel owner rang to say that the other coach had arrived and was ready to swap passengers. They had taken her back to the coach and saw the transfer across the river. We were much relieved. She arrived in Brisbane early Sunday morning and with the driver and a taxi made her way across the City to the NSW coach centre. The rain was still pounding down and many roads were flooded but she finally made it to Lismore to a heroine's welcome at her new school.

By three o'clock that Sunday afternoon in January1974 the Brisbane River burst its banks. With the cyclone and a king tide, Brisbane flooded with the worst floods in living memory. The water reached the first floor of the lovely hotel we had recently stayed in. We were always very thankful that she made it across the city that day as the coach station was flooded up to its roof. Jane-Ann's story across rivers and floods made it into the local paper.

The rain continued on the coast and in the West and again we were cut off. The two main rivers near us flooded for miles and thousands of sheep, cattle and wildlife were drowned. Luckily, Longreach was on a slight hill. Looking out from the Shell Depot on the edge of town the water was up to the lower rungs of the telegraph poles that ran along the side of the rail tracks. I always wish I had taken a photo of it as it is hard to believe just how high the water was. I went up in a little two-seater plane, and as far as the eye could see there was water like an inland sea with little islands of homesteads.

Life in Longreach was not always about flying insects, snakes or poisonous millipedes in the garage. Sometimes it was about nights out dancing or special occasion dinners in the elegant Motel dining room or the New Town Hall. One such occasion was when the Queen had Knighted Jimmy Walker. Now Sir James Walker. We celebrated with great pomp and champagne. Although he had a very large ranch with hundreds of Santa Gertrudis Cattle (originally from the King Ranch in Texas USA!) his house in Longreach was only a few yards away from us and I often chatted to him over his garden fence on my way to work.

Sir James, the Town Mayor and Council decided to have a very English Debutante ball in honour of Sir James's Knighthood. One morning, talking over the fence as he pruned his roses, he asked me to be the Matron of Honour. It was a great evening and we had primary and High School Debs. Nothing quite like it had been done before.

By the middle of our second year we were well immersed in the social and Church life of Longreach. The Anglican Church of St Andrew was also the foundation home of the Bush Brotherhood (begun in 1897). Brothers Keith and Godfrey arrived a few weeks after we did. Like us they had never been in the outback. They helped to form a 'Little Theatre,' a church choir, new services and a growing congregation. The church provided a very small house only just suitable for two people. Neither of them were very good cooks and often came to dinner with us. Brother Keith rang me up one morning asking for help. The Bishop was coming from Northern Queensland to see how they were settling in and to Confirm some of the congregation. They could manage breakfast but could we please feed him dinner? He was coming in two days time.

I had never entertained a bishop before but I had grown up in hotels. I sorted the menu out and now the seating. We had a very large table that came with the house. Lovely for entertaining but I had no suitable large tablecloth. There was only one small general shop so I dashed there. I came away with three yards of cream cotton/linen and one yard of dark mauve furnishing lace. There were eight for dinner so I made eight serviettes and tied them with mauve ribbon, made the tablecloth and squared up the lace and placed it in the centre of the table with cut-glass candle holders and cream candles.

It was a delightful evening with lovely company and a lot of laughter. The Bishop was great company and each time he came to Longreach he would eat with us. We always felt very privileged. Many years later, still using the cream tablecloth, we still referred to it as the Bishop's tablecloth.

Chapter X
A BUILDING FOR A DOLLAR

The small community (about 2,000) of Longreach relied heavily on the social clubs and community groups such as Rotary and Lions. We even had a golf club, played on sand! The children had soccer, cricket, swimming, Scouts, Cubs and Guides to name few. Because many of the children from Sheep Stations stayed in a hostel Monday to Thursday there were a lot of out of school activities. The adults had a town band, fishing, rodeo, golf, bowls (on grass), dog training, jockey and a Polo-Cross club.

I can't stress enough how isolated we were and that making our own entertainment was vital to surviving – 820 miles from the city was one long drive.

Apart from those clubs mentioned there was a thriving spinning and weaving group – we were deep in sheep country – an art group, theatre group, pottery group and a speaking group called 'Forum', much like 'Toastmasters'. What we lacked was a centre where we could all be together.

Just off the main street was an old two-storey ambulance building built in 1921. The underneath had room for ambulances and above had rooms that could house us all. It had lain empty for a few years and the ambulances relocated to the hospital. The old ambulance place was however owned by the Queensland Government and not by the town. Our MP, born in Longreach, was also a friend of Sir James Walker. Between them they petitioned Parliament to grant us a peppercorn rent of one dollar. Government agreed, as long as it was repaired and made safe within one year. Shops donated cement, wood and glass whilst many volunteers, Rotary and Lions clubs members cleared the overgrown vegetation, both inside and out, rewired the electrics, replaced the rotten wood and made it safe. It passed the inspection within the year and so we decided to have a big Art and Craft display and a party.

Now we needed a choir. I went to every church and club inviting singers. I might add that at that time I didn't really understand how very parochial the churches were and never mixed but, with a big smile, I just bowled in and asked. I had over 100 singers and a few from every church including a couple of nuns who sang and taught music. Because I sang in my own church and had a good descant voice the Nuns from the Catholic Church had asked me to sing in their Easter and Christmas services. This I did for the three years we were there and I'm sure it helped to break down the religious barriers. We had about eighty singers in the end. We had a few rehearsals with the Town Band (mostly Salvation Army), and lots of laughter.

A few weeks later we were as ready as we could be. It was my first time conducting so many people and I was terrified. I can't remember what we sang but it went down well. The next morning the last of the cement path was laid and those that had helped set up the centre were asked to leave a foot or hand print.

So, my footprint is forever left in the Paradise of Longreach in the Central West of Outback Queensland. By the end of our time in Longreach it was also the end of my first ten years in Australia. In my wildest dreams Australia had been nothing like I imagined it would be. It also brought the first trip back to England to see my parents, and that changed my life again.

WILD AUSTRALIA

There are stars like burning candles
in a blue black velvet sky,
and only sheep and cattle
to wander by-and-by.

Remember now, the coloured suns
and moons large as melons.
The sweeping birds and raucous parrots
that flash across with talons.

Black floods, white draughts, red fires
all claim this fragile land
with snakes, and flies, and kangaroos
who live among the sands.

It's only man that's changed this world
of wonders still untold.
The Dreaming Time is still the same.
——- Remember this my soul.

Sheilah Daughtree

Acknowledgements

For all my family and friends who encouraged me to write this.

My grateful thanks to Daphne van Loenen
for all the hours spent editing.

Thank you also to Lynn Cooke for her lovely drawings,
to Ian Cooke for reading the early drafts and
to the Writers' L'ink and Malvern Writers' Circle members
who have listened to many of the stories.